Saint Augustine Carriage Tour

Phil King

Saint Augustine Carriage Tour Copyright © 2011 Phil King
Photographs Copyright © 2011 Phil King
Cover Design by Ivy N. King

King, Phil
Saint Augustine Carriage Tour
90 p. 102 ill. cm.
ISBN 978-1-935795-83-4
1. History—United States—Southeast—Florida—St. Augustine.
F306
975.08
Library of Congress Control Number: 2011926768
All Rights Reserved. No part of this book may be reproduced, stored in a retrieval system, or transmitted in any form or by any means, electronic, mechanical, photocopying, recording, or otherwise, without permission in writing from ClearView Press, Inc.
ClearView Press, Inc.
PO Box 353431
Palm Coast, FL 32135-3431
www.clearviewpressinc.com
Printed in the United States of America

Dedication

I'd like to dedicate this book to my two children, Dusty and Sonya, who persevered and became the wonderful and successful people they are today. And to my true love, Bonnie, for her moral and technical help in getting this done. To Yvette Monell, the patient publisher of Old City Life Magazine, where these chapters first appeared. Also, to my many friends who put up with my withdrawal periods for writing. I have been truly blessed.

The Tour

Getting Started	1
The Forts	11
Afterlife	17
Flagler's Churches	24
Flagler's Hotels	30
The Old Village	38
St. Francis Street	46
Heading Back	52
The Plaza	60
Back to the Bayfront	67
Alligator Farm	71
Index	77
Author Biography	81

Introduction

St. Augustine is where it all began. Ponce de Leon discovered the Fountain of Youth, Florida and the United States at the beginning of American History. Pirates and privateers sacked St. Augustine, the Oldest City. Slaves from the Underground Railroad became free here, and then the first free Black settlement defended Spanish Florida. Osceola led American Indians against Andrew Jackson's forces. John D. Rockefeller's silent partner, Henry Flagler, with Thomas Edison and Louis Comfort Tiffany built the finest hotels in the world. Dr. Martin Luther King Jr. was arrested here, and St. Augustine prompted the passing of the Civil Rights Amendment. Ghosts, spirits and orbs still haunt the Ancient City's historic buildings. Join Thorton and I for a tour to see and hear the most colorful and concise introduction to American History.

Getting Started

Welcome to Saint Augustine, the oldest continually inhabited city in our country, and where United States history began. Saint Augustine is also one of the most beautiful and friendly cities anywhere. We'll be traveling about two and a half miles through the historic streets, and it'll take about an hour. But we are on island time, so kick back and take in the scenery.

That's Thorton up front, and I'll let him set the pace since he will be doing most of the work. In fact he can do the whole tour by himself, but he's a little 'horse' today. So, I'll be talking almost non-stop, pointing out things as we go. If you have any questions just ask, and I'll tell you what I know or make up a good story on the spot. The main thing is to relax and enjoy yourselves. I've been a licensed historic guide for six years and spend a lot of time researching my facts, but I never let the truth get in the way of a good story.

Before we get going, let me tell you about a few things that we won't be passing by today, because we are regulated where we can go with a horse and carriage. If you look over the top of the fort ahead, you can see a very tall cross. Just beyond that cross is where it all began.

CROSS OVER FORT

PONCE DE LEON

You remember from your history that Ponce de Leon discovered the Fountain of Youth. Well, just north of that cross is where he found it, back in 1513. Not only did he discover the Fountain of Youth, but also he was the first European of record to set foot on United States soil.

You see, Ponce de Leon, whose name means Prince of Lions, came to the Americas with Columbus in 1493 on his second trip. They landed on Puerto Rico, and Juan Ponce de Leon became its first governor. Columbus

GETTING STARTED

Blue Peacock at Fountain of Youth

Fountain of Youth Segway Tour

never did make it to the mainland. He had heard that there was a Fountain of Youth on the island of Bimini and told Ponce about it. After being forced to turn over the governorship to Columbus' nephew, Ponce set out looking for the fabled fountain. Fortunately he missed the whole island of Bimini and landed about a half-mile north of here, just past the Grand Cross. When he did, he noticed that the Timucuan Indians lived to about 75 years old. Back then, the Spanish lived to 40 or 45 on average. Also, the Timucuan men averaged about 6 foot, 6 inches tall, while the Spanish averaged about 4 foot, 6 inches. In fact, the Timucuan chief was over 7 feet. Naturally Ponce de Leon figured there must be something in the water, so he called it the Fountain of Youth and claimed 'La Florida' for King Ferdinand and Queen Isabella of Spain. Ponce de Leon died at the ripe old age of 47, after being shot in the rear end with a poison Indian arrow over by the Gulf near Ponte Gorda. He died on his way to Cuba in search of medical help. Otherwise who knows how long he would have lived.

TIMUCUAN LIFE

GETTING STARTED

FORT CAROLINE

About 50 years later, King Philip II heard that French Huguenots had built Fort Caroline about 40 miles north of here where Jacksonville is now. Huguenots were French Protestants. After The French Wars of Religion began with the Massacre of Vassay,

MENENDEZ LANDING

Huguenots left France for the America's. In 1564, Huguenot leader, René Laudonnière founded Ft. Caroline, claiming a stake in Spanish territory. King Philip II sent Don Pedro Menendez, his best and most ruthless admiral, here to eliminate the French foothold at Fort Caroline and make the sea safe for Spanish gold ships. Before Menendez arrived, Norman navigator, Jean Ribault, joined Laudonnière at Ft. Caroline with six ships and 600 fighting men.

KISSING THE CROSS

Menendez landed with about 800 settlers near where that 208 foot tall, stainless steel cross now stands. They held the first Catholic mass there and founded Saint Augustine, in the name of God, on September 8, 1565. Archeological evidence shows they began building the town right where the Fountain of Youth is, 55 years before Plymouth Rock and 42 years before Jamestown. Saint Augustine has been occupied ever since. It was named after Saint Augustine, whose feast day it was when they first spotted land. Of course the English wrote our history books, so we weren't taught much in school about the Spanish.

GETTING STARTED

The 208-foot cross was put there in 1965 to commemorate the 400th anniversary of that first mass. In 1964 Hurricane Dora reeked havoc on Saint Augustine, but since the Grand Cross was put there in 1965, we have not been touched by hurricane force winds.

Well, enough of the preliminary facts. Let's get going. Step up Thorton! Time to show these nice people the Old Town.

GRAND CROSS

VIEW FROM CROSS

As Thorton gets moving, let me point out the Intracoastal Waterway with the inlet from the Atlantic Ocean to the right over there. North of the inlet is Vilano Beach with coarse sand and plenty of shells. The Intracoastal Waterway north of Saint Augustine Inlet is known as the North River or the Tolomoto River, named after the Tolomoto Indians who lived in the area. South of the inlet and to my right the Intracoastal is called the Matanzas River. Across the way is Anastasia Island, named after King Philip's daughter. It has 15 miles of beautiful, sugary sand beaches on the ocean side, and you can drive almost the entire length, if your vehicle is capable.

SAINT AUGUSTINE INLET

SAINT AUGUSTINE BEACH

Matanzas means slaughters in Spanish, and the river got its name because of several slaughters of Huguenots by the Spanish. A few weeks after Pedro Menendez arrived here he followed Indian paths about 40 miles north to attack the Huguenots at Fort Caroline. When he arrived, he found about 100 men there taking care of the women and children. He killed the men and let the women and children go. He then went out looking for the rest.

About the same time, the Huguenots were on their way down to Saint Augustine by sea to attack the Spanish. However, their ships were blown south and destroyed by a hurricane between Daytona and Cape Canaveral. The survivors hiked all the way back to the end of Anastasia Island, about 15 miles south of here. That's where Don Pedro Menendez met them. He made a pact with them, took their guns and transported them across the river. He asked them in small groups if they would become Catholic. When they said no, he slit their throats and threw 235 bodies, ten at a time, into the Matanzas River, which ran red for two days. He did this with two major groups of survivors as they made their way north to him. That is why Matanzas is plural. About 19 Huguenots (with trades Menendez needed) did become Catholic, but although their lives were spared, they were put into slavery.

PIRATE MUSEUM

On a slightly brighter note, there is a new Pirate & Treasure Museum on the left here. Pat Croce renovated this building and moved artifacts and displays here from his former museum in Key West. Pat is a motivational speaker, author, and pirate historian filled with energy and creativity and has inspired an enthralling, interactive pirate experience.

This museum connects many of the most well known pirates with the history of St. Augustine. Although they sacked, plundered, and burnt down the town, pirates were also a part of our life and economy through rum running, ship supply, repair and actually residing in St.

Augustine. Pirate enthusiasts are now an increasing share of our visitors.

    I hope you are enjoying the history and scenery so far. We'll be coming to the oldest stone fort in America next. We'll talk about amazing battles with English, Union soldiers, Indians, and plenty of pirates. We'll see century old graveyards populated with ghosts. You will experience some of the finest hotels and hear about the richest people in the world when Saint Augustine was known as The American Riviera. You will hear how Saint Augustine was the destination of the Underground Railroad, and birthplace of the Florida East Coast Railroad which served to build Miami and was extended over the ocean to Key West. We will travel back in time and down some of the most quaint and picturesque streets in the country. Step lively, Thorton.

The Forts

Not *too* fast, Thorton, we're not in a hurry. I love driving Thorton. He has been pulling a carriage for about 12 years now and knows the town as well as anyone. We'll be stopping about half way through the tour, and he'll be glad to give you kisses for carrots. I bring him about two pounds every day. Thorton's got quite a personality. He never gets in a hurry and that gives me plenty of time to tell you the history of this town.

We are approaching the oldest National Monument in the country, Castillo de Saint Marcos. There were nine previous forts in Saint Augustine made out of wood, but insects, fire and pirates destroyed them. British buccaneers, Sir Francis Drake in 1586, John Davis in 1606, and pirate Robert Serles in 1668, all fiercely sacked

Castillo de San Marcos

Saint Augustine and destroyed the wooden forts. That's why Queen Mariana ordered this stone fortress be built.

The Spanish started this impregnable fort in 1672 to protect Saint Augustine Inlet that in turn protected Spanish trade and gold ships from the British and pirates. Soldiers, slaves, Indians and hired craftsmen all diligently worked on it for 23 years. It was completed in 1695 out of coquina, a stone found in only a few places in the world.

Coquina is a natural, local stone made out of tiny shells calcified together for a half million years or so out in the bay. It was mainly quarried near where Saint Augustine Lighthouse is now, and then ferried a couple of miles to the fort. While it was still wet, coquina could be sawed into blocks rather easily, or even molded by hand like clay. But once it dried out it became harder than concrete, and cannon balls would mostly just bounce off.

The Spanish would sneak out at night, pick up the cannon balls, refurbish them in a kiln which is still out back, and fire them back at the British the next day. Sometimes cannon balls would stick into the twelve-foot thick walls. Coquina wouldn't crack like concrete. It just became reinforced with iron.

The fort was painted all white with oxblood red towers. Oxblood mixed with goat milk makes a great paint…just a little hard to find at Home Depot. The Spanish would patch and paint any damage at night, and the bright white fort again appeared ominous and impervious to attackers in the morning sun. The Castillo was under siege many times, but never taken by force.

Seven years after the fort was completed the British, under Carolina governor, James Moore, attacked it for two months, but their cannon balls just kept bouncing off. Finally, in desperation, the British burnt down the entire town while fifteen hundred people and livestock took refuge in the fort. The British finally fled when Spanish reinforcements arrived from Cuba.

Before we move on, it is said that the ghost of Osceola is in the Castillo de San Marcos. He was captured in the Second Seminole War and held here, until he became mortally ill. His doctor took him to a fort in the Carolinas where he got worse and died. His doctor, whose family had died in the Seminole War, asked to be alone with the body and severed his head and brought it back to the fort. I'm told Osceola still roams the fort at night looking for his head.

After Moore's attack in 1702, the Spanish built the Cubo Defense Line from the fort to the San Sebastian River to protect the town. Later the Rosario Defense Line basically went down Cordova Street enclosing early Saint Augustine. These were twelve-foot high walls of palm and had dry moats outside for the cattle when the town was under siege. The spiked plant you see is called Spanish Bayonet, a yucca plant, which surrounded the moat and can give you nasty cuts. So, if anyone tried to attack the town, first they got cut up by the Spanish Bayonet and then were stomped on by the bulls.

SPANISH BAYONET AND CUBO DEFENSE LINE

Saint Augustine Carriage Tour

OLD CITY GATE

The North Gates were built into the Cubo Defense Line wall in 1729, and the coquina pillars were added in 1808. It was outside these gates that the body of ten year old Lizzy was found one cold morning. I guess she didn't get back by evening curfew when the gates closed. She may lightly grab your arm as you go through the gates at night. I wouldn't give her so much credence if she hadn't haunted a fellow carriage driver's home for months. But, she's harmless and just likes to welcome you to the Old City.

THE MILL TOP

Inside the gates, you can see St. George Street, known locally as Credit Card Alley because there are hundreds of shops in which to save money on great buys. If you are hungry, The Bunnery is fantastic for breakfast. Pizzalley's has great Italian food, and The Mill Top is a fun place for lunch or dinner. The Oldest Wooden Schoolhouse is one of the favorite attractions for kids on St. George Street.

OLDEST WOODEN SCHOOLHOUSE

In 1906 the city wanted to tear the gates down in the name of 'progress', but the women wouldn't let them. The women held a tea party there for days, leaving the men without their attentions and pleasures. Finally the men said, "Please ladies, come home…you can have your gates…we need you." They should have known better than to mess with the women's shopping area.

These gates and palm walls, flanked by Spanish Bayonet, were important in 1740 when the British again attacked Saint Augustine under General James Oglethorpe of Georgia. Although Oglethorpe attacked fiercely for about a month, he could not take the fort or the town.

By the way, there is another fort in Saint Augustine about 2 miles north of here called Fort Mosé. It was very important in repelling the attacks of Oglethorpe in 1740. You might say that Fort Mosé was the end of the American Underground Railroad in the 1730's. If slaves could get to Spanish Saint Augustine they became free when baptized as Catholic and promising 4 years service to the Spanish Crown. Fearful of being returned to slavery by the British, the Blacks warned the Spanish and slowed Oglethorpe's advances and also interrupted his supply lines. Unfortunately, Fort Mosé was destroyed in the "Bloody Mosé" battles and not rebuilt for 12 years. Although it was responsible for saving Saint Augustine, only now is it being turned into a state park.

Also, about 15 miles south of Saint Augustine, near the site of the Huguenot massacres, is Fort Matanzas. Small and manned by only seven soldiers, it repelled the British from attacking from the south with only one cannon shot. This free National Monument provides a pleasant boat ride to the fort's picturesque island. The park rangers give a great tour through the fort. A ladder climb to the fort roof provides a wonderful panorama of this almost untouched landscape. It is a perfect excuse for a family ride down A1A on Anastasia Island, and the price is right.

Fort Matanzas

Enough about the forts and wars, next we'll visit a couple cemeteries and a few other places of the dead and maybe some undead. I'll show you a grave that opened one evening before our eyes as a walking ghost tour of about 50 people ran for their lives. Then we will tour amazing churches, hotels and hear how they enhanced Old City Life.

Afterlife

Now that we've talked about the forts, wars, Fountain of Youth and the Grand Cross, it's time to turn left onto Orange Street and back into some of our town's darker history. Step up Thorton. Let's keep a quick pace through here. Good horse, I won't call you Pokey Man, anymore.

HUGUENOT CEMETERY

Across from the Old City Gates we have the Huguenot Cemetery. Huguenot means French Protestant, as we talked about in the first part of the tour. Although there are few Huguenots buried here, it is mostly just Protestants.

In 1821, the United States bought Florida from Spain for five million dollars. For about the same price as one nice beach house today, they got the whole state. Also during 1821, there was a Yellow Fever outbreak. Nearly 500 people died. The Catholics could be buried inside the city, but there was nowhere to bury the non-Catholics. They were burying people where the fort lawn is and anywhere they could. That is why the United States set aside the Huguenot Cemetery so that anyone could be buried there.

I've been told that all that they buried then weren't really dead…they just looked that way. When they dug up some of the bodies to put them into the new cemetery, they found scratch marks inside some of the coffins, as if they were trying to get out. It's said that they began tying a string around the wrist and up to a bell. If the bell rang, a watchman would cry, "There's a dead ringer!" Of course, the one who monitored the bells at night was on the "graveyard shift".

I'm not sure if this is where that story got it's beginning, but I can tell you if you take pictures at night here, you are apt to get an awful lot of 'orbs' in those pictures. They say those are the energy of the spirits. If you take night pictures in the rear of this cemetery, you are likely to see a woman's face on one of the graves amongst the orbs.

Enough of that stuff, I'm giving myself the creeps. Coming up on the right is our beautiful, new four-story parking lot. I love the

CITY PARKING LOT

clock. Looks a lot more like a fancy hotel or a convention center, doesn't it? It opened 4th of July Weekend, 2006 and helped relieve the parking here somewhat. Of course they had to raise the price of parking to pay for it, but that's helped scare some tourists away and create even more spaces.

As we round the corner here onto Cordova Street, you see the Authentic Old Drug Store, and I know that because it has four signs on it. It's made of cypress and cedar. Both are great at repelling bugs, so they can get away without painting it. Most of the medicines of the 1800's didn't really cure much, but they sure made it so you didn't care.

AUTHENTIC OLD DRUGSTORE

Next we have the Love Tree Café. Notice the palm tree growing out of and being hugged by the live oak tree. They say if you kiss your loved one under it, your love will endure forever. So be careful whom you kiss here.

LOVE TREE CAFE

Coming up is the Tolomoto Cemetery, named after the Tolomoto Indian village that was here. In 1763 England beat Spain in the Seven Years War over in Europe. The Treaty of Paris gave Florida

TOLOMOTO CEMETERY

to England, and the Spanish were forced to move to Cuba. The Tolomoto and the last hundred Timucuan Indians, who had not died of European diseases, went with the Spanish since they were their friends and had become Catholic. That's when they turned this into a Catholic cemetery. Slowly, let your eyes scan the trees here for the spirit of a boy who often hides in the Spanish moss and can be seen sitting in the branches. The line of white head stones is for Confederate soldiers. Most of the rest of the graves are above ground since hands and feet tend to float to the surface with a ten-foot deep water table.

You'll notice the fresh cement on the sarcophagus next to the Civil War head stones. Near Halloween 2004, we came through here just after dark. Nearly fifty people listened intently as their ghost tour guide told them about the ghosts here. Suddenly, we heard a resounding crash as that grave exploded, and everyone ran for his or her life. Thorton bolted in fear, and our carriage patrons screamed as we thankfully charged away, leaving the mayhem behind. Many men left chivalry in their past as they outran their dates. It wasn't until daylight that I could see the hefty oak branch that fell down on the grave that night.

Do you see the mausoleum in the back? There was a bishop who had died and was being viewed at the Cathedral through a glass coffin top when his decaying body exploded from the heat. They picked up the pieces and brought them in cloth bags to the little mausoleum you see back there. Finally his body was sent to Cuba, but they say he still haunts the place looking for his missing wooden teeth.

Saint Augustine has a lot more than ghosts. We have about 28 romantic bed and breakfasts. Be sure to contact one for the Bed and Breakfast Tour in December. You will be delighted by the quaint inns, antiques, and charming décor while you meet the owners and get acquainted with the vacation getaways available right here in town.

Saint Augustine Carriage Tour

Casa de Suenos

Carriage Way

One of those wonderful inns is Casa de Suenos, here on the corner. Its name means House of Dreams, which is appropriate since this was formerly a funeral home. However, there are no ghosts here. They have the finest accommodations decorated with treasures that the innkeeper, Kathleen Hurley, has acquired from around the world. Special packages and carriage tours are offered.

Another fine inn is Carriage Way Bed and Breakfast. It dates back to 1883, built by Edward Masters who would become one of Henry Flagler's lead carpenters for his first hotel in St. Augustine. Larry and John Johnson ran the inn with their father, Bill, since their parents bought it in 1992. Their mother passed away before it opened, and their father passed away recently. Larry and John continue the fine B&B experience today. In keeping with their Carriage Way theme, they have recommended carriage tours, and we have picked many up at their inn for special occasions. Their guests have always highly complimented the Carriage Way and its keepers.

I promise I will leave the spirits alone, as we begin the next leg of our tour. You will hear a great deal about Henry Flagler, John D. Rockefeller's original partner in Standard Oil. I'll tell you about the railroad, churches and hotels that he built here. He transformed Saint Augustine and all of Florida, as he attempted to bring Riviera style life to this quiet historic town. His three wives, three children, partners and competitors will be brought to life and often dragged through the dirt, as I tell you how Saint Augustine came into its modern age.

Flagler's Churches

Now that we've made it through most of the goblins and ghosts, we are approaching the part of town that I feel has some of the most interesting architecture, inspired by some of America's most influential people. We are stepping into the history of the 1880's and a town dominated by Henry Flagler, famous hotelier, railroad tycoon and the oil baron partner of John D. Rockefeller.

Henry Morrison Flagler was born the son of a poor Presbyterian minister in Upstate New York. The name Morrison was his mother's first husband's last name. Henry worked his way to Ohio on the new Erie Canal at age 14. There he stayed with his half brother, Dan Harkness, from his mother's second husband and worked for the Harkness family store, becoming manager in about a year. He married his step-uncle's daughter, Mary Harkness, and they had two daughters, Carie who died at age 3, and Jennie Louise, and one son, Harry.

After losing $100,000 in a salt business at the end of the Civil War, Henry went into a grain and distillery business and paid back his debts. He then borrowed $100,000 from a Harkness family member to partner with John D. Rockefeller and start Rockefeller, Andrews & Flagler Oil Company that became Standard Oil…. BP/Amaco to you kids. Rockefeller considered Flagler the brains behind the operation because of his secret rebate contracts with the railroads that made Standard Oil a monopoly. Achieving that status, Henry retained his seat on the board, but left the world's largest corporation for new horizons.

Henry Flagler came to Jacksonville, Florida with his first wife, Mary Harkness, as was recommended by her doctor for tuberculosis.

Although they took a side trip to Saint Augustine, Henry didn't enjoy the Old City at that time. Unfortunately, Mary Harkness succumbed to TB after going back to New York.

Flagler returned to Florida on his honeymoon with his second wife, Ida Alice Shrouds. They fell in love with St. Augustine but found the accommodations sorely lacking. Henry combined several railroads, making them standard gauge, and created the St. Augustine based 'Florida East Coast Railroad'. Once connected with New York and the world, Flagler began to build his hotel empire and create the American Riviera.

GRACE UNITED METHODIST CHURCH

While Flagler started his first hotel, he built the beautiful Grace United Methodist Church out of poured concrete in 1886 as an exchange for a swamp bound church right where he wanted to build his second hotel. Fast and long-lasting, poured concrete allowed him to quickly build beautiful buildings, still solid a hundred and twenty some years later.

Since he helped the Methodists, Flagler gave the Baptists the land and helped them raise ten thousand dollars to build the first yellow brick structure in the area, called the Ancient City Baptist Church. He had only two requests: complete it in two years, and no bells in the steeple. You see, Henry's church was on the next corner, and he didn't want any competition with the Baptists on Sunday morning. I won't tell the joke about the No Bell Prize.

ANCIENT CITY BAPTIST CHURCH

Unfortunately, Henry Flagler's daughter, Jennie Louise, became ill and depressed after loosing her baby, Margaret, only three hours after she was born. Henry invited her, and she was coming here from up North on her in-laws' yacht, accompanied by her husband, Frederick Benidict, and her brother, Harry Flagler. However, when it pulled into Charleston, South Carolina she was found dead.

Henry was devastated and wanted the Memorial Presbyterian Church built for the one-year anniversary of his daughter's death. He hired one thousand artisans who worked 24 hours a day in two twelve-hour shifts, because Henry offered them triple the normal fifty-cent per day wage. They completed the entire building in only 361 days. You couldn't get a building permit in that amount of time today. It had temporary windows like the one in the east door now, when it opened.

MEMORIAL PRESBYTERIAN CHURCH

The wonderful stained glass windows, you see now, depicting the Apostles Creed, took twelve years to be completed by Herman Schladermundt, a German friend of Tiffany in New York.

Memorial Presbyterian is also made of poured concrete in the shape of a Roman Cross and based on St. Marks Cathedral in Venice. It has a 150-foot high copper dome topped with a brass cross. The spires, called finials, are of white terra cotta. Inside, the pews are of mahogany with marble inlaid flooring. The organ is one of the largest and finest in the country with over 5,000 pipes. This church is open 9 to 4 daily for a free tour, so take your time and enjoy it. Be sure to check out the mausoleum. I'll give you the dirt on all this when you come out.

FLAGLER MAUSOLEUM

In the meantime I'll give Thorton a drink, and you can feed him some carrots when you get back. Okay, Thorton, take a break and have some water. Yes, I have the carrots.

Welcome back. Thorton's been waiting for you. Here, take a whole carrot and show it to him. Then touch your cheek and say, "Give me a kiss, Thorton," when he grabs the carrot, just let him have it. I hate picking up pieces of fingers.

Did you notice the empty grave in there? Henry is on the right, his daughter, Jenny Louise, with baby Marge in her arms are next to him. Then his first wife, Mary Harkness, is on the left-center next to their daughter. The grave on the left is empty. Many say it was for Henry's son, Harry. When Henry's wife, Mary Harkness, had TB, Henry got 'awful close' to her nurse, Ida Alice Shrouds, and he ended up marrying her. They lived on the other side of the church in a place called Kirkside where Ida Alice threw big parties like the Queen of

Saint Augustine. Henry's son, Harry, didn't like this. After running Henry's three hotels here for a year, they fought, and Harry permanently moved to New York in 1895 taking his mother's maiden name and never speaking to his father again. As Harry Harkness, he married into the Lamont family, wealthy New York publishers. He went to Columbia University and became a successful banker and cofounder of the New York Philharmonic Society which supported the orchestra.

However, according to the church historian, the empty coffin was for Henry's third wife, Mary Lilly Keenan of the North Carolina Keenans. When Henry died in 1913 at age 83, she inherited about 113 million dollars, becoming one of the wealthiest women in the world. But when she remarried, she became ineligible for the grave. I guess that she must have eaten too much of her new husband's cooking since she soon died of arsenic poisoning (the results of the autopsy were never released). Fortunately she had a prenuptial agreement and her new husband only got five million. He was tried for her murder, but since she used European makeup with arsenic in it, and arsenic was used to treat syphilis in those days, he got off. So, her husband, named Bingham returned to Ohio with five million, minus lawyer's fees. I think he had Johnny Cochran as his lawyer.

You ask, 'What happened to his second wife?' I'll tell you soon, as we pass her room in the old Ponce de Leon Hotel, which is now Flagler College. We'll also talk about two other Flagler hotels and how he got the Casa Monica for next to nothing.

Are you done with your carrot time, Thorton?

Flagler's Hotels

Y ou've all heard about Henry Flagler being John D. Rockefeller's original partner in Standard Oil. This is where he came to create a winter paradise for the wealthiest from New York and the world. We are coming up to Flagler College, originally known as the Ponce de Leon Hotel when it opened January 10, 1888. I say it was the finest hotel in the world partially because of the smokestack in front of us. That stack was built by Thomas Edison to produce DC electricity in two oil-fired generators at its base. One of the generators is now in the Smithsonian. Edison also designed the two

EDISON'S SMOKESTACK

ornate towers as water towers. The Ponce de Leon was the first hotel in the world to have hot and cold running water and electricity in every room. Electricity was so new, they had to hire special servants just to turn on and off the lights.

PONCE DE LEON HOTEL

Also, young Louis Comfort Tiffany was the interior decorator of the Ponce de Leon, and the largest collection of his stained glass still adorns the dining room where Flagler students eat most of their meals. The robin's egg color of Tiffany Blue still dominates the décor while carved woodwork sets the ominous tone of this restored masterpiece. Magnificent murals by renowned George Maynard portray the splendor of the American Riviera period. The building was designed by young architects Hastings and Carrere and constructed out of poured concrete.

PALM CROQUET COURSE

The palms you see on the west side of the hotel were planted two by two in the shape of a croquet course, so women of the day could play croquet in the shade. Back then, the whiter they were, the wealthier they were. They even wore lead-based makeup laced with arsenic to make them whiter (notice I didn't say wiser). The chain on the fence is a replica of the chain stretched by the Spanish across the inlet to keep out invading ships.

Only the most prominent families were invited to stay at the Ponce de Leon. It was only open January, February and March and suites were rented by the season. Often the husband would take care of business in New York when necessary by commuting a day and a half on the luxury trains. The same carriage company you are riding on today would taxi the guests to and from the depot 122 years ago. I've heard it is the oldest business in Saint Augustine, started back in 1879.

Let me tell you about Henry Flagler's second wife, Ida Alice Shrouds. It is said that she had threatened Henry's life and was locked up on the third floor here. Although it was illegal to divorce an insane spouse, it became legal for only three months when Henry had a special session of the Legislature called. After the divorce Ida Alice spent the rest of her life in a New York asylum supported by Henry. Of course, some say that red haired Ida still stalks around at night dressed in a white gown, carrying a candle, and scaring a few students.

Across the street is the unique Villa Zorayda. Franklin Smith, an amateur architect from Boston, and the founder of the Y.M.C.A. built it as his home in 1883. The Moorish revival building, a $1/10^{th}$ scale replica of a portion of the Alhambra Palace in Granada, Spain, was important as the second building ever to be made of the new and enduring 'poured concrete'. Flagler built most of his buildings in Saint Augustine with it.

VILLA ZORAYDA

The Villa Zorayda reopened a few years ago filled with magnificent antiques, some being thousands of years old. You'll notice that every window in the Moorish Revival building is different. They say that once the building was cleansed of evil spirits, those spirits became so confused they could not find their way back in. Oh, and the strange lettering you see above the front door is Arabic for "Only God conquers all."

ALCAZAR HOTEL

We are coming up on Flagler's second hotel, the Alcazar, across the street on the right. It was built on the swamp that Henry traded the Methodists for and filled in. It is now City Hall and the Lightner Museum, but in 1888 Henry built it for the working class. However, it was also the play place for the rich and famous. It had a two-lane bowling alley, state of the art gym/spa and the world's largest indoor swimming pool. It also housed Florida's largest casino, which in those days meant entertainment or dance hall rather than gambling parlor.

ALCAZAR SPA

Flagler's Hotels

One of my favorite places to relax is the courtyard garden with ponds filled with huge Koi.

ALCAZAR POND

The swimming pool stretched from Cordova Street to Granada Street. It was the center piece of the luxurious life of the wealthy guests. It is still there, but it has been drained and is now a gourmet restaurant. It is open daily, but only for lunch. This is surrounded by an antique mall in the pool peripheral under the floors above.

CAFE ALCAZAR POOL

In 1948, Otto C. Lightner, the Chicago publisher of "Hobby Magazine", turned the old Alcazar into a museum for his Eclectic Victorian collections from around the world. You never know what you might find in that amazing mix.

CASA MONICA HOTEL

Step out, Thorton. I want to show these nice people the luxurious Casa Monica on the left as we come around the corner. Franklin Smith, the same guy who built the colorful Villa Zorada, built this using the poured concrete he introduced. Unfortunately, this caused plumbing problems with the pipes that were incased in it. Adding to Smith's woes was Flagler's desire to eliminate competition as he did with Standard Oil. So, when people were on the way south on Flagler's trains, he more or less told them, 'We don't mind if you stay at the Casa Monica, but if you do, you can find your own way back to New York.' After only three months, and only renting out three suites, Franklin Smith sold the Casa Monica to Henry Flagler for a fraction of what he had in it. Henry called his third hotel the Cordova, like the name of the street we are riding down.

The Cordova was conveniently connected to the Alcazar by an over the road passage when Henry ran it as a hotel until the depression.

It eventually became the St. Johns County Court House in the sixties until the county built its new complex north of town. In 1999, the Kessler Corporation bought it and turned it back into a luxury hotel and used the original name, The Casa Monica.

Next, Thorton will be taking us back through important places of the Civil War and Civil Rights. I hope you know where you are going Thorton, cause we are following you.

The Old Village

Step up Thorton, it's time to move this carriage down the page of history. As we leave the grand hotels of Flagler's era, you'll notice Palm Row on your left. These were the houses of well to do snow birds of the Flagler era. With duplicated simplicity and close proximity to grandeur, these modest two story wooden houses gave frequent visitors a place to call home in the South.

Palm Row

On the left, sitting back from our road, you will see St. Joseph's Convent. It was built in 1884, and the Vatican donated the statue you see of 'Jesus and Child'.

ST. JOSEPH'S CONVENT

As we continue down Cordova Street, we come upon Dow Museum of Historic Houses, previously known as Old St. Augustine Village. On this site, the first hospital in the continental United States was built in 1597. Of course it is gone today, but there are nine homes here constructed between 1790 and 1910. They were bought up in the 1950's by Kenneth Worcester Dow (no relation to the chemical company) who turned them into a historic museum mainly of the 1800's. In 1863, the Emancipation Proclamation was read on these

OLD SAINT AUGUSTINE VILLAGE

grounds, freeing all the slaves in Florida. Many freed slaves went about two blocks west of here and started Lincolnville, a historic Black community of today.

M L KING STAYED HERE

In fact, just a block away and a hundred years later, Dr. Martin Luther King Junior began protest marches from his Florida headquarters of the Southern Christian Leadership Conference on Washington Street. King sent children to march through town, because so many adults had been beaten in marches here previously.

THE RECORD

THE OLD VILLAGE

Racial tensions were so intense then that State Police even fought against County Deputies when Blacks integrated the beaches. We'll talk more of that later, but the Record building before us was where these stories were reported, or not, to the world. It now provides apartments for college students, as the newspaper has moved to the edge of town.

Turn left here, Thorton. We'll go down Bridge Street behind the St. Augustine Village. By the way, there hasn't been a bridge on Bridge St. since Flagler filled in the Maria Sanchez Creek and swamp to build his Alcazar Hotel. I love the gates behind the museum here, but

FIRST GATE

SECOND GATE

you have to be over 18 to look into this first one, because of those nudie statues. There's John in the window of the second gate. He does a wonderful job taking care of the neat old buildings and beautiful flowers and loves to watch the horses go by.

PRINCE NAPOLEON MURAT'S HOME

The pink colored house at the end of the 'Village' was built in 1790 of coquina and was home to Prince Napoleon Murat, nephew of Napoleon Bonaparte. He later married the grand niece of George

ST. JOSEPH'S RETIREMENT HOME

THE OLD VILLAGE

Washington. Exiled from France at the end of Uncle Napoleon's reign and his father's execution, Crown Prince Napoleon Murat boarded here many times between 1824 and 1834. He became a good friend of fellow boarder, Ralph Waldo Emerson. Just to drop another name, Greta Garbo dined here when it was a restaurant in 1939.

Whoa, Thorton, let me point out the Sisters of St. Joseph retirement home here on the corner of St. George Street. Sorry, I can't let you off to visit no matter how much you loved those sweet, old teachers, heh-heh.

Across the street is the Cathedral Parish Elementary School. St. Joseph's High used to be back here also, but it was moved to the edge of town. There are some neat old houses back here, but first look at these bricks in the street.

REYNOLD'S BLOCKS

Step out, Thorton. The story has it that these 'Reynolds Blocks' were made in Scotland by R. J. Reynolds as ballast to replace the weight of tobacco shipped to Europe. Flagler got a good deal on them from Reynolds and brought them down on his trains, so the city could pave the streets to his hotels. Although the city didn't want to pave the streets, Henry just kept piling them up in the Plaza. Finally, in response to Henry's pressure, they paved streets, but only the one-way streets leading away from his hotels.

UPHAM WINTER COTTAGE

Meanwhile, with investment from Flagler, Henry Plant was paving the streets of Tampa with Reynolds Blocks. Plant built the railroad and hotels down the West Coast of Florida while Flagler dominated the east. The grand Tampa Bay Hotel is now the main building of the University of Tampa and the counterpart to Flagler College. Plant City is named after him.

Before we turn on to St. Francis Street, I want to turn you on to some of the beautiful architecture on the back streets. One of my favorite homes is the 1893 Upham Winter Cottage. If this was a cottage, I'd like to see their regular home. This Queen Anne Victorian home has 7 bedrooms and 5+ baths. With 5800 square feet of space, it is on sale for less than 1.2 million. Better speak up soon. Too bad I don't get commission.

The Old Village

HIBBARD HOUSE

Next door is the Hibbard House with a widow's watch up top, so the wife could watch for her husband coming back from sea.

Stay on board for the next chapter as we talk about the most haunted inn, the oldest house, the Florida National Guard, unknown soldiers, the exodus of the Cherokees and more. In the meantime Thorton says, "Just turn the page when you are ready."

St. Francis Street

You'd think that after about twelve years of pulling a carriage in this town, Old Thorton here would have gotten used to everything, but his ears still perk up when we head for the St. Francis Inn. Built back in 1791, it is well renowned as one of the most haunted bed and breakfasts in the country. The St. Francis Inn has been on national TV many times because of its ghosts. In fact, the most authentic ghost story in St. Augustine was verified to us on this carriage, when we met a half dozen excited paranormal investigators here who said their meters read way off the charts.

St. Francis Inn

Almost everyone who works here has experienced Lilly at least once. She was a servant girl and fell in love with the owner's nephew. His father wouldn't let him marry her, so she hung herself right up top there in the first room on the left, 3A, now known as Lilly's Room. Her lover killed himself a short time later when he found out about her death. However, both have been experienced quite often since then.

When a disconcerted worker asked at the front desk who the strange woman on the third floor was, they simply said there was no one up there. But, when he described her, they told him it must be Lilly. That explained her strange appearance and eerie occurrences in her room. This and more was told to me by his wife and verified by his son.

St. Francis Inn is loaded with charm and friendly personnel like Ellie who has shared many stories with me and those on our carriage. It's a wonderful place to stay and reasonably priced, but it may take over a year to reserve Lilly's room.

Come on Thorton, let's head down St. Francis Street toward the bay front. On our right is the Fernandez-Llambias house, constructed in the early 1700's. Originally a one story, two room coquina house, the British style second story and porch were added in the early 1800's. It still has the outside kitchen like most houses back then.

FERNANDEZ LLAMBIA'S HOUSE

Saint Augustine Carriage Tour

TOVAR HOUSE

On the left is the Tovar House. Until recently this was a great museum of Florida's military history. Unfortunately, all the weapons, uniforms and other authentic artifacts were removed recently by the National Guard for unknown reasons, and the empty museum was closed.

Part of the same complex, The Oldest House, owned by the Historical Society and known as the González-Alvarez House, is next and tells the history of early St. Augustine. Digs through its floor unearthed a thatched roof shack of the early Spanish Period. A house built here around 1650 was burnt down in 1702 when the British, under General Moore, burnt the entire town down. The present house was

THE OLDEST HOUSE

built of coquina by Thomas Gonzalez between 1715 and 1727 as a simple two room home. When the British were here between 1763 and 1784 the second story was added. Eventually the porches and other additions made it as it stands today.

There are 5 flags flying here today. The first is from the First Spanish period from 1565 to 1763. The second flag is British. They won the Seven Years War in Europe and got Florida by the 1763 Treaty of Paris, and the Spanish had to go to Cuba. The Spanish helped

INSIDE THE OLD HOUSE

America beat the British in the American Revolution and got Florida back in the 1783 Treaty of Paris. Therefore, the third flag is of the Second Spanish Period which lasted until 1821 when United States bought Florida from Spain for five million dollars. The U.S flew the fourth flag until the Civil War. Then in 1861 to 1862 the Confederate flag flew, but does not fly here now. In 1862 the United States flag flew again.

Until the British came, there were no doors facing the street. You entered from within the walled compound, so they could tell if you were friend or foe. When the British made the monastery into a barracks, the Oldest House owners put doors on the street and invited the soldiers to come to their pub for an ale.

SAINT FRANCIS BARRACKS

The yellow building across the street from the Oldest House is now the Headquarters of the Florida National Guard. It was originally the convent of the Franciscan monks who converted the Indians to Catholicism in the late 1500's. When the British came here they turned it into the Saint Francis Barracks, and it has been military ever since. The first building was probably of wood, but after St. Augustine was burnt down in 1702, it was rebuilt out of coquina. The Spanish did not allow the use of coquina, until the fort was completed in 1695.

Also on the National Guard property is the King's Bakery where bread was baked during the British period. Across from that are officers quarters with a national cemetery next to them.

THE KING'S BAKERY

In the National Cemetery, among the traditional white crosses, three pyramids entomb 1,468 unknown soldiers from the Second Seminole Indian War of 1835 to 1842. This is when Osceola led the remnants of all the displaced tribes from the North against superior US forces. Although outnumbered, Osceola fought desperately to resist extinction.

St. Francis Street

OFFICER'S QUARTERS

The Indian Wars were basically when the Indians were rounded up and sent on the famous "Trail of Tears" to the "End of the Trail" in Oklahoma. By that time, Osceola had been captured, held at Castillo de San Marco here, and then transferred to the Carolinas where he died a natural death.

Okay, Thorton, let's head back up the waterfront, and we'll tell these nice people about the lighthouse, tour boats, marina and the Bridge of Lions, etc. on our next leg. No wonder I call you Pokey Mon, it's taking a year to finish this tour. Maybe we'll have to turn it into a book. Yes, Thorton, I'll put you on the cover.

NATIONAL CEMETERY

Heading Back

Okay Thorton, now that we've shown them the Oldest House, St. Francis Barracks, and the National Cemetery, it's time to head back to the carriage stand where I'll have a few more carrots for you. To save a little time let's do a U-turn up here. Just remember, if anyone says anything, it was your idea, or you can forget those carrots.

Well folks, across the Intracoastal Waterway you can see the St. Augustine Lighthouse. It was completed in 1874 and is 165 feet tall with 219 steps you can climb to the observation walkway around the red lantern.

It is identifiable to sailors by the red cap and black/white diagonal stripes. It is powered by a 1000-watt light bulb and has a first order Fresnel lens. At night it is identifiable up to 25 miles at sea by a flash every 30 seconds.

The lighthouse has been on the "Ghost Hunter's" TV show, which had many encounters with the paranormal there. The story I've heard the most is about the old light-keeper who had a heart attack carrying a 10 gallon can of lamp oil up the 219 steps. Of course he still haunts those steps at night. There are plenty of other stories about that place, but I don't want Thorton up all night with bad dreams, again. But, if you are really into ghosts, I'm sure you have seen them on TV.

Heading Back

Saint Augustine Lighthouse

Saint Augustine Carriage Tour

SOUTH ANCHORAGE

This portion of the Matanzas River is known as the South Anchorage, because it's south of the bridge. It has changed recently. It was one of the last frontiers until about a year ago. Boaters could stay here for free with no time limit. Just drop anchor out of the channel and call it home. 'Sort of like the Old West. Now they are assigned a mooring ball for a few hundred dollars a month. The good side is that includes the right to park a dinghy at the marina and shower privileges that they had to pay for before. Plus there are water taxis and refuse pump out boats now. It only costs a hundred or so more a month, but it is a way of life disappearing. It doesn't sound like much to us landlubbers, but it is history and freedom being rewritten in a town of boaters. What was free is now under government control.

MUNICIPAL MARINA

Speaking of freedom, let me tell you about some people who moved to St. Augustine in 1777. The Minorcans, which included people from Minorca, Greece and Italy, came to New Smyrna (south of Daytona) as indentured servants at an indigo dye (blue violet plant from India) plantation. However, they were mistreated and pretty much enslaved. They complained to the British who were in power at that time. The British rescued them, and the Minorcans followed them to Saint Augustine where they have a great presence and culture very evident here today. If you get a chance, try some Minorcan clam chowder with locally famous datil pepper.

THE LIONS

The Bridge of Lions is one of Saint Augustine's most remarkable landmarks. It opened to traffic in 1927 as the Matanzas River Bridge but was renamed the Bridge of Lions. Dr. Andrew Anderson II commissioned a pair of 5000 pound Lions to be sculpted by F. Romanelli of Florence, Italy. Although Dr. Anderson died in 1924, when the Lions arrived in 1927 the bridge was renamed the Bridge of Lions, honoring Ponce de Leon, the Prince of Lions.

There was a major controversy almost ten years ago, whether to rebuild it or

BRIDGE UNDER CONSTRUCTION

RENEWED BRIDGE OF LIONS

replace it with a four-lane high rise bridge. The locals and tourists alike loved the historic bridge. That is why it was rebuilt, using the original copper-steel spans and the Mediterranean Revival towers, instead of being replaced by a modern structure. Construction started in 2005 and was completed in 2010.

The restaurant on the pier ahead is the Santa Maria. In 1763 a landing was built for ships to load. It was rebuilt in 1885 and after Hurricane Dora in 1964, moving somewhat over the years. It was bought by the Connell's and remains in the Connell family today. Perhaps its most famous claim to fame is the invitation to feed the fish and birds as you eat.

SANTA MARIA RESTAURANT

Next is the St. Augustine City Marina where you can dock your yacht or embark for romance, thrills, education, ghost or pirate encounters.

Eco Tours has catamarans or inflatable powered boats (pictured on previous page in front of the Santa Maria pier) for visiting dolphins, waterfowl, manatees, turtles, marine habitats and other wild life. Captain Zach McKenna will share his zeal for nature with you.

The Black Raven is a 72-foot, 1700's style Spanish Galleon owned by Gunnar Hedqwist. A crew of bawdy pirates host scheduled tours, weddings and other charters complete with an interactive, raucous comedy show. Historic accounts of local pirates at sea add nicely to the other great nautical tours of St. Augustine.

BLACK RAVEN PIRATES

BLACK RAVEN

For a romantic or ghost tour, the Freedom is a two-mast top sail schooner that will enchant you with a feeling of yesteryear. They even exchange cannon fire with the fort.

FREEDOM

A scenic cruise on the Victory III is a relaxing way to learn the history of the town on the water from Mike Usina. His family has run tour and ferry boats here for over a century. In fact, the bridge to Vilano Beach is named after his grandparents who ran a ferry before the bridge was built. When I took my brother and his girlfriend on the Victory III they were thrilled by more than 30 dolphins, as we toured the Matanzas and Salt Run near the Lighthouse. Locals should check out the great specials for residents.

VICTORY III

The Smile High Parasail boat is here every summer to give you a thrill by dangling you over the ocean and landing you right back on the boat.... if you're nice.

O.C. WHITE'S

Coming up on the left is one of my favorite restaurants, O.C. White's. According to his brother Gary, Dave White got the nickname O.C., meaning out of control, from his best-forgotten adventures as a pilot. But O.C. White sounds like a good old fashion pirate to me.

O.C. White's was originally built in 1790, as one of the first St. Augustine Hotels. Once known as the Worth Mansion, it was eventually bought by George Potter of Florida's first Wax Museum. In 1961, the entire stone building was moved across the street, and I'm told it was a Wendy's before the scrumptious cuisine of today. Dave White has done so well with it that he now owns all the way up to King Street.

HEADING BACK

BELLA BAY & J.P. HENLEY'S

His green building contains Bella Bay, a five room Historic Inn. Also, J.P. Henely's is one of our finest pubs with about 100 bottled and 50 draught beers or ales.

A block down Artillery Street is Denoel French Pastry Shop renowned since 1966. Even though it is a block off the tour, I better point it out, because its reputation keeps people asking me where it is.

Finally, the big yellow building on the corner is the A1A Ale Works. Originally it was the Surprise Department Store. Then, as Potter's Wax Museum, "The House of Wax" was filmed there with Vincent Price in 1953. Nowadays, A1A Ale Works is an excellent restaurant and microbrewery. In the same building, there are

DENOEL FRENCH PASTRY

great shops, an art gallery, ice cream parlor, and the Habana Village Café with live Latin jazz. Also, Dave White tastefully remodeled the large White Room for big weddings and parties.

Okay Thorton, it's time to stop at the famous "Long Light". For a whiff of what's coming up, we will be talking more about the bridge, 'Slave Market', Cathedral, the short guy, tallest building and the race Thorton won.

A1A ALE WORKS

THE PLAZA

The picture of the bicycle race reminds me that Thorton really wants me to tell you about the race he won. He's not known as the fastest horse, but he did have his claim to fame one night by the Plaza de La Constitution.

This crazy guy, David, pulled up alongside our carriage with a silly contraption known as a conference bike, a round red bike with six passengers and a driver who all peddle. "Get a horse!" I said.

"You wanna race?" David snarled.

"You got it!" I replied, and I felt Thorton get all excited.

When the light changed, off we went. Thorton reared up and

BICYCLE RACE

lunged forward. In the meantime, the stunned peddlers grabbed the lead, momentarily, until Thorton took the race seriously and hit his stride, while our passengers cheered him on. Like a champion, he passed the bicyclists in the stretch and by the time we got to Harry's I had to pull back on the lines, so we didn't all go to jail. Ol' Thorton strutted with pride for a month and still sneers when he sees a bicycle. It proves one horsepower is more than seven panting people power.

Now that I've stroked Thorton's ego, I better tell you about all these things around the Plaza.

First of all, this Plaza de la Constitucion is the oldest public park in America. It was laid out by the Spanish Royal Ordinances in 1573. Each colony was to have a plaza such as this for public gathering. The first Standard of Weights and Measures in the country was established here when the market was created in 1598. An 1812 monument remains today which commemorated the new Spanish Constitution. All such monuments in the Spanish colonies were ordered destroyed when the liberal Spanish Constitution was repealed. This is the only one left in the Western Hemisphere. Only the inscribed tablets of the constitution were removed.

1812 CONSTITUTION MONUMENT

The market building is known as the "Slave Market". The town doesn't like this name, but there is still a sign on it saying it got the name during the 20 year British Period ending in 1784. The British started a lot of plantations in the area and probably used a lot of slaves. This particular building was constructed in the 1840's and rebuilt after the fire of 1887 left only the stone pillars.

Although this has been a market place for over 400 years, the city has tried to stop the artisans from displaying wares. The artisans have gotten an injunction against the city, but the courts still must rule further.

SLAVE MARKET

In the circle in front of the Plaza, the little statue is Ponce de Leon, who discovered and claimed Florida for Spain in 1513. It is an exact replica of the one in San Juan, Puerto Rico, where he was the first governor until Columbus replaced him with his nephew.

Ponce de Leon was only 4 foot 11, and that's probably with his hat on. And he was the tallest on his ship.

THE PLAZA

PONCE DE LEON

The seven story building on the right of the Plaza is the Wachovia Bank. After it was built as the First National City Bank in 1929, the townspeople decided they didn't want a bunch of skyscrapers and limited all future construction to 35 feet, or three stories. That regulation remains a key to our city's charm.

WACHOVIA BANK

CATHEDRAL DE BASILICA

The church you see next to the bank is the Cathedral de Basilica. It was completed in 1797, and rebuilt with Henry Flagler's help after the 1887 fire. They say the congregation is the oldest in the country, dating back to 1565 when the first American mass was held where the big cross is now.

At the far end of the Plaza is the Government House. Since the early 1600's until after United States bought Florida in 1821, Saint Augustine governed the Eastern half of Florida here, while Pensacola governed the West. After 1821 they located a site in the middle and built Tallahassee as the new Capitol. Due to age and fire, the Government House was rebuilt several times. In the 1930's, the W.P.A. constructed this building based on the 1764 British Governor's house.

The Plaza

Government House

It has served as Post Office, Courthouse, Customs and city offices. It is now Saint Augustine's Department of History and the Downtown Visitor Center.

On King Street, to the left of the Plaza, is the Trinity Episcopal Church. It was Florida's first Episcopal church, opening in 1831, and is renowned for its wonderful bells that fill the city with music every day, and also for its Tiffany stained glass window. The congregation does some wonderful and kind work there today, and I think it would rather forget its segregationist stance during

Trinity Episcopal Church

the Civil Rights Movement.

Speaking of which, the old Woolworth store stands next to it. This too had a discrimination role and was the scene of protests and sit-ins at the lunch counter. But, today is today and you can still see "Woolworth's" on its large door handles.

Old Woolworth Store

POTTER'S WAX MUSEUM

A couple of doors east of Woolworth is Potter's Wax Museum. This was the first wax museum in Florida and is a great rainy day excursion into the past with its prominent characters. When the museum was where the A1A Ale Works is now, it had the title role in the movie, "The House of Wax" with Vincent Price.

As we continue down Avenida Menendez, there are a couple of renowned local watering holes. First, at Tradewinds Tropical Lounge, actually on Charlotte Street, there's always a good time waiting for you. Be ready for a razzing though as Matanzas, who plays there daily, likes to stir things up. I'm told this is where Jimmy Buffet got his start.

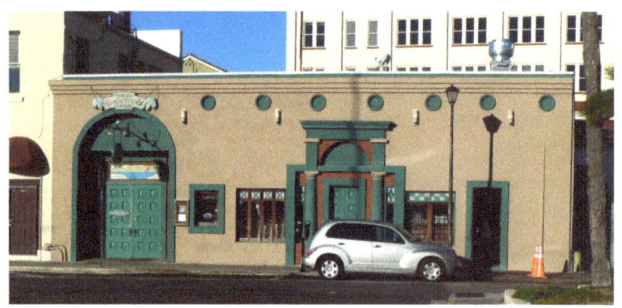

TRADEWINDS TROPICAL LOUNGE

He used to play here for drinks, but he drank more than he played, and they told him he would never make it. So, off he went to Margaritaville.

Close by is the American Legion. Although its flagstaff celebrates the victory of World War I, the Legion is better known for its low key and low cost drinks and meals. It is open to the public.

AMERICAN LEGION

Back to the Bayfront

Before we get moving down Avenida Menendez toward the Carriage Stand on the last leg of our tour, let me just mention two places across the Bridge of Lions. O'Steen's Restaurant, famous for its exceptional shrimp, is just a few blocks down on the right. The Conch House is a few blocks further. Take a left after the Sunrise Inn. You'll find the Conch House Marina Resort with tiki top tables, fine dining, great music, yachts, fishing charters, pelicans, and amazing views. It's a place not to be missed.

Now, let me point out some of these beautiful old buildings, as we head down the bay front. The red building on our left is Harry's Restaurant. They have excellent New Orleans style food there and a

Harry's Restaurant

beautiful patio in which to dine outside. But if you go to the Lady's Room upstairs, you are very likely to meet up with Catalina. Although you may not see her, you are apt to feel her presence very strongly. I told this to one carriage group and a woman told

HILTON HOTEL

me, "That explains why two years ago I was up there and I had the weirdest feeling ever in my life. I didn't know until you just told me that it was haunted."

You see, Catalina do Porras was born in that house and lived there for 10 years before the British took over Florida in 1763. The Spanish returned in 1784, but it took her five years to recover her childhood home. Six years later she died, but she still refuses to leave. Even though it was burnt down in 1887, it was rebuilt in 1888 to its original specifications, and she still remains along with a man in a black suit. Ask anyone who works there about all the coincidental and mysterious happenings.

Next we have the Hilton Hotel. No, those are not old buildings. This is brand new construction, opening just days before the Super Bowl was held in Jacksonville in 2005. The City Historic Board negotiated with Hilton to ensure that it would fit well with the old architecture around it. Although it looks like colonial houses on the outside, inside it is almost like a regular hotel, and even has a two story parking lot below with six pumps to keep the sea water out. It is far different than what it replaced.

STEPS WHERE M.L. KING WAS ARRESTED

The Monson Hotel, which stood here, was demolished in 2003. The only remnants are some steps, now in the central parking area. Those steps are where Dr. Martin Luther King was arrested in 1964. Although the Monson owner, James Brock, employed and served blacks as well as whites, Klan threats and bombs forced him to change his policy. When Dr. King came to be served, he was turned away and a disturbance ensued, which resulted in King's arrest. The press served to enhance the civil rights movement, and one week later protesting blacks and whites jumped in the pool. Distraught by forced confrontation, Brock poured in pool chemicals, and police jumped in to arrest the intruders. The photo of Brock was on the front page of papers around the world. Two weeks later the historic Civil Rights Bill was signed by President Johnson on July 2, 1964, thanks in part to what happened here in St. Augustine. For more information, check out St. Augustine's Freedom Trail, online or with one of their tours.

Next to the Hilton is the Casablanca, often voted the Best Bed and Breakfast in town. This Mediterranean Revival inn dates back to 1914. With the Prohibition Act being passed in 1919, it became the boarding house of choice for Treasury agents when they were in town. The aging woman innkeeper knew some rumrunners who would drop anchor in view of the inlet. If there were no agents she would swing a

CASA BLANCA BED & BREAKFAST INN

lantern on her widow's walk. By 1933 and the end of Prohibition the innkeeper was a millionaire, thanks to her rum-running friends.

Well, we are back where we started, and Thorton says it's time to take a break. I want to thank you for riding with us, and I hope you had a great time. We do accept tips, but Thorton prefers them as carrots and apples. Be careful getting down and enjoy your time in St. Augustine.

As Thorton slurps his water, I'm going across the street to Mary's Harbor View Café for a cup of coffee. That's where the drivers take their breaks. It's one of the favorite breakfast and lunch stops for locals and tourists alike. It's also one of the best values in town for unique food and modest prices. Stop in for an ice cream cone and get to know Mary and the gang. It's one of the friendliest places in town. Tell them Phil sent you.

And come on back the next time you are in town. You are only a stranger once.

MARY'S HARBOR VIEW CAFE'

WHAT'S NEXT?
ALLIGATOR FARM

Oh, let me recommend a couple of things for you to do tomorrow. Take Florida Highway A1A across the Bridge of Lions about a mile and visit the Alligator Farm and Zoological Park. Not only do they have hundreds of alligators, they have many other exotic animals there, with interactive exhibits.

The all natural wild bird rookery is simply amazing. Herons, Egrets, Wood Storks, Ibis and its cousin, the pinkish Roseate Spoonbill are just a few of the many wetland birds that can be easily viewed at the St. Augustine Alligator Farm. These birds often live and raise their young in nests just out of arm's reach. It is a favorite place in the country for professional and amateurs to get some fantastic bird pictures. The bird pictures in this chapter were taken at or near the Alligator Farm.

The reason so many birds nest there is they are attracted by the safety alligators provide by eliminating nest robbing predators like

ALLIGATOR

ASIAN CROCODILE AND TURTLE

raccoons, opossums, and snakes. Unfortunately, older chicks push weak or younger ones out of the nest, rewarding the alligators below while upholding the strength of the species through survival of the fittest. Being a natural habitat, birds are not contained, fed or interacted with.

The Alligator Farm has just opened Crocodile Crossing, an aerial adventure and obstacle course in the tree tops with seven zips over the zoo! Comedian Jimmy Fallon said, "An alligator farm in Florida just installed a zip line visitors can ride above the alligator tanks. It's like the alligator version of a sushi bar with one of those conveyor belts."

Another place you might want to visit is the St. Augustine Lighthouse & Museum. The easiest way to get there is follow the road at the end of the Alligator Farm across A1A to the Lighthouse. There you can climb the

ZIP LINE OVER ALLIGATORS

219 steps to the top of the lighthouse for a magnificent view. There is also a great maritime museum to educate you on lighthouses and maritime facts past and present in St. Augustine.

Sample of Birds at Alligator Farm

WOOD STORK

PELICAN

Saint Augustine Carriage Tour

Great Egrets

Cattle Egret

Wood Ducks

Alligator Farm

Blue Heron

Saint Augustine Carriage Tour

Roseate Spoonbills

INDEX

A
A1A Ale Works 59
Alcazar Hotel 34, 36, 37, 41
Alhambra Palace 33
Alligator Farm & Zoo 71-76
American Revolution 49
American Legion 66
Anastasia Island 8, 9, 16
Andrew Anderson MD II 55
Apostles Creed 28

B
Baptist, Ancient City 26
Bimini 4
Bella Bay 59
Benedict, Frederick 27
Birds, Alligator Farm 71-76
Black Raven 57
Blacks 15, 40, 55
Bonaparte, Napoleon 42
BP/Amaco 24
Bridge of Lions 51, 55, 71
Bridge Street 41
British 12, 15, 16, 48-50, 55, 62, 64, 68
Brock, James 69
Buccaneer 11
Buffett, Jimmy 66
Bunnery 14

C
Cape Canaveral 9
Casablanca 69
Casa Monica Hotel 29, 36, 37
Capitol of Florida 64
Casino 34
Castillo de San Marcos 11, 12, 51
Cathedral de Basilica 21, 59, 64
Cathedral Parish School 43
Catholics 6, 15, 18, 21, 50
Charleston, SC 27
Cherokee 45
Chicago 36

City Gates 14, 17
City Hall 34
Civil War 24, 31, 49
Civil Rights 37, 65, 69
Columbus, Christopher 2, 4, 62
Confederate 21, 49
Cordova Hotel 36, 37
Coquina 12, 42, 49, 50
Croce, Pat 9
Crocodile Crossing 72
Cross, Grand 1, 2, 4, 6, 7, 17, 58
Cuba 12, 21, 49
Cubo Defense Line 13, 14

D
Daytona 9, 55
Datil pepper 55
Davis, John 12
Denoel French Pastry 59
Dolphins 58
Dow, Kenneth Worcester 39
Dow Museum of
    Historic Houses 39
Drake, Sir Francis 11
Drug Store, Old 19

E
Eco Tours 30, 31
Edison, Thomas 30, 31
Egrets 71
Emerson, Ralph Waldo 43
English 6, 10, 21
Erie Canal 24
Emancipation Proc. 40

F
Ferdinand, King 4
Fernandez-Llambias Hs 47
First National City Bank 63
Flagler,
    College 29, 44
    Family 4, 24, 25, 27, 29

INDEX

Henry 23-27, 30, 32, 36, 43, 44, 64
Florida East Coast RR 10,25
Fort Caroline 5, 6, 8
Fort Matanzas 16
Fort Mose´ 15, 16
Fountain of Youth 2, 4, 17
Franklin Smith 33, 36
Freedom, Tall Ship 57
Freedom Trail 69
French Wars of Religion 5

G
Garbo, Greta 43
Gates, Old City, North 14 17
Georga 15
Ghosts 10, 12, 14, 8, 21, 23, 24, 47,68
Gold 12
Government House 64
Grand Cross 1, 2, 4, 6, 7, 17, 58
Greece 55
Gulf (of Mexico) 4

H
Habana Cuban Restaurant 59
Harkness, Dan, Mary 24, 25, 29
Harry's Restaurant 60, 67
Herons 71
Hibbard House 45
Hilton Hotel 68
Historical Society 48
House of Wax movie 59, 66
Huguenots 5, 8, 9, 16, 17, 18
Hurricane 7, 9

I
Ibis 71
Indian Wars 4, 8, 10, 12,20, 21, 50, 51
Intracoastal Waterway 8,52
Italy 55

J
Jacksonville 5, 25, 68
Jamestown 6
Jimmy Fallon 72
Johnson, President L. 69
J. P. Henely's 59

K
Keenan, Mary Lilly 29
Kessler Corporation 37
King Ferdinand 4
King, Dr. Martin Luther 39, 69
King Philip II 5
King's Bakery 50
Kirkside (Flagler home) 29
Ku Klux Klan 69
Key West 10

L
Laudonnier, Rene' 6
Leon, Ponce de 2, 29,30-32 55, 63
Lighthouse 12, 51-53, 72
Lightner, Otto, Museum 34,36
Love Tree Café 20

M
Marie Sanchez Creek/ L. 41
Marina, Municipal 51, 54, 57
Mary's Harbor View Café 67
Massacre of Vassay 5,
Matanzas 8,9,55,58
Maynard, George 31
Mediterranean Revival 56, 69
Menendez, Pedro 6, 8, 9
Methodist Church, Grace 26
Miami 10
Milltop Tavern 14
Minorca 55
Monson Hotel 68
Moore, General James 12, 13, 48

INDEX

Moorish revival 33
Murat, Prince Napoleon 42, 43

N
National Cemetery 50, 52
National Guard 45, 48, 50
New Orleans 68
New Smyrna 55
New York 24-25, 28-30, 32, 36
North Carolina 29
North (City) Gates 14, 17
North River (Tolomoto) 8

O
O.C. White 58
Oglethorpe, James 15
Ohio 24, 29
Oldest House 45, 48-50, 52
Old Wood Schoolhouse 14
Osceola 12,13,50,51

P
Palm Row 38
Pirates & Museum 9-12
Pizzalley's 14
Plant, Henry and City 44
Plazza de la Constitución 61
Plymouth Rock 6
Ponce de Leon 2, 29, 30,-32,50, 55, 62
Ponte Gorda 4
Potter, George 58, 59
Poured Concrete 28, 36
Presbyterian, Memorial 27, 28
Price, Vince 66
Prince of Lions 2
Prohibition Act 69
Protestant 5, 17

Q
Queen Isabella 4
Queen Mariana 12

R
Renolds Blocks (R.J.) 43, 44
Ribault Jean 6
Rockefeller, John D. 23-24, 30
Rockefeller, Andrews & Flagler Oil Company 24
Rookery, Alligator Farm 71
Roseate Spoonbill 71
Rosario Defense Line 13

S
Saint Augustine 1, 6, 7, 9, 10, 12, 15, 16, 25, 40, 48
Saint Marks Cathedral 28
Saint Johns Court House 37
Saint Joseph Convent 39, 43
Saint Francis Barracks 50, 52,
Saint Francis Inn 46
Salt Run 58
San Juan, Puerto Rico 62
Santa Maria 56
Shladermundt, Herman 28
Scotland 43
Seminole 50
Seven Years War 20
Shrouds, Ida Alice 25, 29, 30, 32, 33
Smile High Parasailing 57
Slave Market 59, 62
Southern Christian Leadership Conf. 40
Spanish 4, 6, 12-15, 18, 21, 48-50, 61, 62, 68,
Standard Oil 23, 24, 30, 36
Super Bowl 68
Surprise Dept. Store 59
Swimming Pool 34

T
Tallahassee 64
Tampa 44
Tiffany, Louis Comfort 28, 30, 31,

INDEX

	65
Timucuan	4, 21
Tolomoto	8, 20, 21
Tovar House	48
Trade Winds Lounge	66
Treaty of Paris	20, 49
Trinity Episcopal Church	65

U

Underground Railroad	10, 15
United States	1, 18, 39, 49, 50, 64
Unknown Soldiers	45, 50
Upham Winter Cottage	44

V

Vilano Beach	8, 58
Victory III	53
Villa Zorayda	33, 36
Vincent Price	59
Visitor Info. Center	65

W

Wachovia Bank	63
Wax Museum, Potters	58, 66
White Room	59
Woolworth Store	65
Worth Mansion	58

X

Y

Z

Zip Line	72

Author Biography

Phil King was a Base Photographer in the Air Force where he did pictures for the SR-71, the fastest plane in the world. He taught photography at the State University of New York at New Paltz where he got his Bachelors degree. Phil drove a horse and carriage for three years and remains a licensed Saint Augustine tour guide.

Phil King recently retired from three years as case manager of the St. Francis House homeless shelter. He remains a monthly history writer for Old City Life magazine and member of Saint Augustine Historical Society. This book is based on a series of his articles in Old City Life magazine.

We Love You Thorton

Thorton passed away at the age of 27 on April 29, 2011, as we were preparing his book for print. He had been retired on a farm for several years where he ran happily in the fields. "Pup Pup", as he was known to many, will be remembered by all whose lives he touched. He has gone off now to be with "Princess", his best friend in the sky. We love you Thorton.

www.ingramcontent.com/pod-product-compliance
Lightning Source LLC
Chambersburg PA
CBHW041219070526
44584CB00001B/18